BIBLEOLOGY

BIBLEOLOGY

THE LITTLE BOOK OF
BIBLE TRIVIA

STAN CAMPBELL

Faith Words

New York Boston Nashville

Unless otherwise indicated, Scripture quotations are from the
HOLY BIBLE: NEW INTERNATIONAL VERSION®.
Copyright © 1973, 1978, 1984 by International Bible Society.
Used by permission of Zondervan Publishing House. All rights reserved.

Quotations noted KJV are from the King James Version of the Bible.

FaithWords
Hachette Book Group USA
237 Park Avenue
New York, NY 10017

Visit our Web site at www.faithwords.com.

Printed in the United States of America

First Edition: September 2007
10 9 8 7 6 5 4 3 2 1

The FaithWords name and logo are trademarks of Hachette
Book Group USA.

Library of Congress Cataloging-in-Publication Data
Campbell, Stan.
Bibleology : the little book of Bible trivia / Stan Campbell.—1st ed.
p. cm.
Summary: "A lighthearted and entertaining book of Bible trivia that's fun
no matter what your age or how much you know about the Bible."—
Provided by the publisher.
ISBN-13: 978-0-446-58052-6
ISBN-10: 0-446-58052-X
1. Bible—Criticism, interpretation, etc.. 2. Bible—Miscellanea. I. Title.
BS511.3.C36 2007
220—dc22
2007015312

Contents

CONTENTS

Introduction

This is not a book for Bible scholars. If you have a wall covered with theology/divinity degrees or have devoted a long lifetime to the examination of every detail tucked among the thousands of lines of Scripture, thanks for your interest, but you can put this book back on the shelf.

Rather, this book is for people who may actually know very little about the contents of the Bible. Those who will get the most out of it are people who want to learn more—who are willing to ponder what they already know and look up new bits of information they discover.

This book was written with the hope that the user will have a pleasant experience reviewing his or her knowledge of Bible "trivia" (an unfortunate word, because I would not suggest that any portion of the Bible is by any means trivial). In fact, I haven't done my job if you don't stop periodically and think, *I didn't know* that *was in the Bible!*

So don't approach this book of Bible "trivia" with the expectation of regurgitating facts you already know. Instead, may you enjoy a voyage of discovery to see what *else* is in the Bible to add to your existing knowledge. You are likely to find that many "trivial" portions of the Bible still contain significant life lessons for those of us trying to navigate our lives in the twenty-first century.

A short book like this can't cover everything in Scripture, but great effort has been made to include many of the usually overlooked portions in addition to most of the favorite sections. And the content is presented in a number of different formats (multiple choice, matching, true/false, etc.) to provide a variety of learning methods as you go through. It is hoped that you will occasionally chuckle at what you find in addition to having a number of "aha" moments throughout this book.

In fact, if you don't find yourself having fun as you go through this little book, you'd better double-check . . . you might be a Bible scholar.

BIBLEOLOGY

1

Identify the Quote

The Bible is the source of many of our everyday quotes and references. For example, when you hear people speak of "the writing on the wall" or a "doubting Thomas," they are using biblical references (whether they know it or not).

Below are a number of familiar sayings. See if you can identify which ones come from the Bible and which have other sources. (And give yourself extra credit if you can identify those sources.) To maintain a similar cadence, the King James Version is used for the Bible verses below.

---

(1) "I am escaped with the skin of my teeth."

(2) "The quality of mercy is not strained, it droppeth as the gentle rain from heaven upon the place beneath: it is twice blessed; it blesseth him that gives and him that takes."

(3) "Can the Ethiopian change his skin, or the leopard his spots?"

(4) "Lord, what fools these mortals be!"

(5) "To everything there is a season, and a time to every purpose under the heaven."

(6) "God helps them that help themselves."

(7) "To err is human, to forgive divine."

(8) "It is more blessed to give than to receive."

(9) "Whatsoever ye would that men should do to you, do ye even so to them."

(10) "For fools rush in where angels fear to tread."

(11) "Pride goeth before destruction, and a haughty spirit before a fall."

(12) "Hope springs eternal in the human breast."

(13) "The love of money is the root of all evil."

(14) "Train up a child in the way he should go: and when he is old, he will not depart from it."

(15) "Spare the rod, and spoil the child."

2

It's a Miracle!

When you think of miracles in the Bible, it's natural to think of Jesus right away. Yet a number of other people either initiated a miracle or participated in one. Some were instruments of God who brought about the miracle; others merely benefited from it. Try to match the following miracles with the people associated with them (listed at the end of the chapter).

Miraculous Event

(1) Interpreted another person's dream without even being told what the dream was

(2) Sat on a hillside during a battle; as long as his hands were uplifted, the Israelites would win, but when he lowered his hands, they would lose (He also parted the Red Sea, struck a rock and had water gush out, and did a lot of other miraculous stuff)

(3) Was bitten by a deadly viper; when he didn't die, the people thought he must be a god

(4) Thrown into a fiery furnace so hot it killed those tossing them in, yet he and his two friends came to no harm

(5) Called down fire from heaven that consumed a drenched sacrifice, the altar, and even the stones and the soil

(6) Exhausted after killing one thousand Philistines with the jawbone of a donkey, he prayed and God created a spring of water right where he was

(7) Used only 300 soldiers to defeat an enormous enemy army

(8) Summoned thunder and rain during the dry season as a sign for the Israelites

(9) Stood before Pharaoh as he (not Moses) changed his staff into a snake, turned the waters of the Nile River to blood, summoned frogs to cover the land, and initiated a plague of gnats

(10) An angel escorted him out of a maximum security prison without anyone noticing until long after he was outside

(11) As a sign that God had answered someone's prayer, this prophet prayed that the shadow of the sun would reverse itself on ten steps of a stairway—and it did!

(12) Because his victorious army was about to see the enemy escape into darkness at the end of day, he commanded the sun to stand still; as a result, "the sun delayed going down about a full day"

(13) Performed many miracles during his life (making an iron axhead float, curing leprosy, bringing a young man back from the dead, etc.); but even after death, when a fresh corpse happened to come into contact with his bones, the dead man came back to life

(14) He and Peter were approached by a beggar who had been crippled from birth; instead of giving him money, they healed him.

Peformed the Miracle

(A) Aaron

(B) Daniel

(C) Elijah

(D) Elisha

(E) Gideon

(F) Isaiah

(G) John (the apostle)

(H) Joshua

(I) Meshach

(J) Moses

(K) Paul

(L) Peter

(M) Samson

(N) Samuel

3

Who Knows His Moses?

The story of the life of Moses fills four books of the Bible: Exodus, Leviticus, Numbers, and Deuteronomy. Below are twenty questions covering just a few of the events of Moses' life. See how much you know about this fascinating Old Testament figure.

(1) When the Moses story begins, the Israelites had been in Egypt for about:

(A) Four years
(B) Four decades
(C) Four centuries
(D) Forty days and forty nights

(2) Moses escaped early death due to clever parents, God's protection, and:

(A) Egyptians with bad aim
(B) Dumb luck
(C) An accounting error
(D) A thrilling escape on an "ark"

(3) After being fished out of the Nile, Moses had a pretty smooth life until:
(A) Egypt lost a big war
(B) A woman cut his hair
(C) A famine hit
(D) He killed a guy

(4) After fleeing to the wilderness, Moses acquired:
(A) Flocks and herds too numerous to count
(B) A wife, a kid or two, and a call from God
(C) A bad attitude
(D) BO like you wouldn't believe

(5) God spoke to Moses from a burning bush and told him to:
(A) Don't just stand there; get some water!
(B) Start working out because times were about to get tough
(C) Go tell Pharaoh he was going to lead the Israelites out of Egypt
(D) Lead the Israelites out of Egypt without Pharaoh finding out

(6) Which of the following was *not* a sign God gave Moses to use if needed?
(A) Producing frogs from nowhere
(B) Changing his staff to a snake and back
(C) Turning water to blood
(D) Giving himself leprosy

(7) After Moses' first request to leave, Pharaoh forced the Israelites to make bricks without:
(A) Limit
(B) Pay
(C) Straw
(D) Bathroom breaks

(8) So God sent a series of plagues. Which of the following are *all* among the ten plagues on Egypt?
(A) Nile turns to blood, body boils, rats
(B) Frogs, flies, the Mummy returns
(C) Darkness, hail, lesions on animals
(D) Gnats, locusts, anthrax

(9) Which of the following holidays was instituted during the Exodus?
(A) Yom Kippur
(B) Hanukkah
(C) Passover
(D) Kwanzaa

(10) Which of the following was *not* taken along in the exodus from Egypt?
(A) Six hundred thousand men plus women and kids
(B) Silver, gold, and Egyptian plunder
(C) A mummy
(D) Lots of freshly baked, high-rise bread

(11) How did the Israelites know where to go?
(A) God showed them continually, day and night
(B) Bright yellow Egyptian road signs marked the way

(C) They knew the general direction of the Promised Land and took as straight a path as possible
(D) God gave them clear instructions prior to leaving

(12) After Moses parted the Red Sea, the last words of the Egyptians are:
(A) "Nah! Those walls of water aren't going to fall on us!"
(B) "Let's get away from the Israelites! The LORD is fighting for them against Egypt."
(C) "Who fears the God of Israel?"
(D) "Onward for the glory of Pharaoh!"

(13) In the wilderness, God fed his people *manna,* which literally meant:
(A) "Heaven bread"
(B) "Honey dew"
(C) "Tastes great, less filling"
(D) "What *is* this stuff?"

(14) Which was *not* a way God (through Moses) provided water for the Israelites:
(A) Moses turned a pool of rancid water sweet by tossing in a piece of wood
(B) God led the Israelites to an oasis of twelve springs and seventy palm trees
(C) Moses hit a rock
(D) Moses spoke to a rock

(15) While Moses was receiving the Ten Commandments from God atop Mount Sinai, the people were:
(A) Supporting Moses with prayer and fasting
(B) Feasting and joyfully praising God
(C) Going about their daily business
(D) Building a new, more accessible god

(16) The gold for the golden calf came primarily from:
(A) Ore found near Sinai
(B) Egyptian tombs
(C) Earrings
(D) Peoples defeated during the Exodus

(17) Before entering the Promised Land, Moses sent in spies who returned with:
(A) Milk and honey
(B) Pomegranates, figs, and one monster cluster of grapes
(C) Livestock
(D) Giant grasshoppers

(18) Ten of the twelve spies recommended turning back due to the immense size of the inhabitants. The people rebelled and God had to intervene to prevent them from stoning the few remaining faithful people. But one thing God *didn't* do was:
(A) Suggest he kill them all and let Moses start over with a fresh bunch
(B) Sentence them to forty additional years wandering the desert

(C) Exempt Joshua and Caleb (the only two faithful spies) from his sentence on Israel

(D) Strike the unfaithful spies with a plague

(19) Moses was allowed to look into the Promised Land but not set foot there because:

(A) He was disobedient and lacked trust in God

(B) He chose to stay on Sinai, in God's presence

(C) He was becoming old and weak

(D) He was voted out of the tribe

(20) Moses was more _____ than anyone else on the face of the earth.

(A) Righteous

(B) Faithful

(C) Humble

(D) Patient

4

Not a Handsome Fellow

The Bible contains some breathtakingly beautiful passages. Then again, in other places are descriptions of some not-so-lovely things. Match the rather pathetic description below, taken straight from the Bible, with the appropriate person (listed at the end of the chapter).

Biblical Description

(1) "He had often been chained hand and foot, but he tore the chains apart and broke the irons on his feet.... Night and day among the tombs and in the hills he would cry out and cut himself with stones"

(2) "A rawboned donkey lying down between two saddlebags"

(3) "Afflicted ... with painful sores from the soles of his feet to the top of his head. Then [he] took a piece of broken pottery and scraped himself with it as he sat among the ashes"

(4) "A beggar ... covered with sores and long-ing to eat what fell from the rich man's table. Even the dogs came and licked his sores"

(5) "A huge man with six fingers on each hand and six toes on each foot—twenty-four in all"

(6) "Red, and his whole body was like a hairy garment"

(7) "He had no beauty or majesty to attract us to him, nothing in his appearance that we should desire him. He was despised and rejected by men, a man of sorrows, and familiar with suffering. Like one from whom men hide their faces he was de-spised, and we esteemed him not"

(8) "A wild donkey of a man; his hand will be against everyone and everyone's hand against him"

(9) "Like whitewashed tombs, which look beautiful on the outside but on the inside are full of dead men's bones and everything unclean"

(10) "He was driven away from people and ate grass like cattle. His body was drenched with the dew of heaven until his hair grew like the feathers of an eagle and his nails like the claws of a bird"

(11) "Under a curse and driven from the ground.... A restless wanderer on the earth"

(12) "'By this time there is a bad odor, for he has been there four days.'...The dead man came out, his hands and feet wrapped with strips of linen, and a cloth around his face"

Character Described

(A)   Cain

(B)   Esau

(C)   Ishmael

(D)   Issachar (One of the twelve sons of Israel)

(E)   Jesus (Based on an Old Testament prophecy)

(F)   Job

(G)   Lazarus (a friend of Jesus)

(H)   Lazarus (a figure in one of Jesus' parables)

(I)   King Nebuchadnezzar of Babylon

(J)   The Pharisees

(K)   An unnamed man with an evil spirit

(L)   An unnamed Philistine

5

We Three Kings

The combined kingdoms of Israel and Judah had only three kings before they split: Saul, David, and Solomon. Each of the three is remembered for both the good and the bad events of his life and kingdom. See if you can identify the correct king associated with each of the following clues:

(1) Committed murder to cover up an act of adultery

(2) Known as "a man after God's own heart"

(3) A head taller than any of the other Israelites

(4) Built and furnished a permanent, magnificent temple for God

(5) Almost had his son killed for eating a little honey during a battle

(6) Once offered one thousand burnt offerings to God

(7) Had seven hundred wives and three hundred concubines, which proved to be his downfall

(8) Experienced both the Spirit of God who allowed him to prophesy and an evil spirit sent from God to torment him

(9) Had a son known for courageous victories against the Philistines

(10) After committing a sin, witnessed an angel standing between heaven and earth, bringing a deadly plague

(11) Accumulated so much wealth that silver was as common in Jerusalem as stones

(12) A wife once scolded him for acting foolishly (he was dancing as worship while underdressed), and she remained childless as a result

(13) Was looking for lost donkeys when he was anointed king

(14) Ordered that the child of a prostitute be cut in half, which resulted in much awe and admiration from the people

(15) Consulted a medium (witch) rather than God and committed suicide not long afterward

(16) Had one son who raped a half-sister and another son who tried to overthrow the kingdom

(17) Could not keep warm when he got old, so a young virgin was hired to be his bed buddy

(18) People from all nations visited just to hear what he had to say

(19) The only one not credited with writing a psalm

(20) Used as a reference by Jesus in his Sermon on the Mount

6

Complete the Psalm

It's the hymnbook of Scripture, a prayer book, and the longest book in the Bible. Psalms is also quoted more in the New Testament than any other Old Testament book. The 150 psalms contain a wealth of literature that is both applicable and memorable. Below is a sampling of quotes from the Psalms. See how well you do at choosing the correct option to complete each thought. But a word of warning: the various psalmists were very honest about their feelings. As you check your answers, you may be surprised at some of the things that are actually stated in the Bible.

(1) Blessed is the man who does not walk:
(A) Where his feet should not tread
(B) In the counsel of the wicked or stand in the way of sinners
(C) Away from the Lord
(D) Around in the temple when he should sit quietly

(2) O Lord, how many are my foes! How many rise up against me! . . . Arise, O Lord! Deliver me, O my God!:

(A) Provide your protection from all my enemies

(B) Forgive my enemies for their offenses against me

(C) Strike all my enemies on the jaw; break the teeth of the wicked

(D) Give unto me a life of peace and prosperity

(3) O Lord, do not rebuke me in your anger or discipline me in your wrath. . . . I am worn out from groaning:

(A) All night long I flood my bed with weeping and drench my couch with tears

(B) Yet I groan no longer for you are with me

(C) But you do not bless groaning, so I laugh instead

(D) And when you groan, the whole world groans with you

(4) Arise, O Lord, let not man triumph; let the nations be judged in your presence:

(A) Let your loving mercy shine on them

(B) Declare them "Not guilty by reason of insanity"

(C) Judge them with complete fairness

(D) Strike them with terror, O Lord; let the nations know they are but men

(5) The Lord examines the righteous, but the wicked and those who love violence his soul hates. On the wicked he will:

(A) Rain fiery coals and burning sulfur

(B) Rain frogs, lice, and plagues aplenty

(C) Reign in power and majesty

(D) Rein in their evil outreach

(6) How long, O LORD?

(A) How long is a cubit?

(B) How long may I continue to serve in your holy temple?

(C) How long must I endure the slings and arrows of outrageous fortune?

(D) Will you forget me forever? How long will you hide your face from me?

(7) The fool says in his heart:

(A) "Two plus two is five."

(B) "God will love me no matter how I behave."

(C) "I am in control of my life."

(D) "There is no God."

(8) The earth trembled and quaked, and the foundations of the mountains shook; they trembled because [God] was:

(A) Almighty

(B) Absent

(C) Angry

(D) Active

(9) May the words of my mouth and the meditation of my heart:

(A) Stave off the forces of evil

(B) Be pleasing in your sight, O LORD, my Rock and my Redeemer

(C) Keep me from getting into trouble

(D) Remain as pure as the newly fallen snow

(10) Even though I walk through the valley of the shadow of death, I will fear no evil, for:
(A) You are with me; your rod and your staff, they comfort me.
(B) Your power goes before me and your love follows wherever I go.
(C) Whatever happens, I am yours.
(D) I am the biggest, meanest son of a gun in the valley.

(11) Who may ascend the hill of the LORD? Who may stand in his holy place?
(A) He who has clean hands and a pure heart
(B) He whose great deeds are known throughout the land
(C) He who is strong in faith and steadfast in good character
(D) He who asks nicely

(12) My guilt has overwhelmed me like a burden too heavy to bear:
(A) Behold! It squasheth me like a bug
(B) Draw near and lighten the load I carry
(C) Remove this weight and I will serve you forever
(D) My wounds fester and are loathsome because of my sinful folly

(13) God is our refuge and strength:
(A) Who guides us safely through the wilderness
(B) An ever-present help in trouble
(C) Whose mighty works are known to the ends of the earth
(D) Who never turns his back on those he has chosen

(14) Surely God is good to Israel, to those who are pure in heart. But as for me, my feet had almost slipped; I had nearly lost my foothold. For I envied:
(A) My neighbor's shiny new chariot with its new-chariot smell
(B) The strength and power of the nations around me
(C) The arrogant when I saw the prosperity of the wicked
(D) The righteousness of the patriarchs of old

(15) O LORD God Almighty, how long will your anger smolder against the prayers of your people?
(A) We beseech you seeking compassion and forgiveness
(B) Without your loving mercy, we fall faint and never arise
(C) The loss of your presence is too much to bear
(D) You have fed them with the bread of tears; you have made them drink tears by the bowlful

(16) I would rather be a _____ in the house of my God than dwell in the tents of the wicked.

(A) Scorekeeper

(B) Doorkeeper

(C) Floor Sweeper

(D) Bookkeeper

(17) The length of our days is seventy years—or eighty, if we have the strength:

(A) And beyond that, eternity with you

(B) Yet our years are but sand through your hands, O LORD

(C) May our lives honor you from cradle to grave

(D) Yet their span is but trouble and sorrow, for they quickly pass, and we fly away

(18) Unless the LORD builds the house:

(A) Its builders labor in vain

(B) It will never withstand the storm

(C) His people continue to wander as sheep without a shepherd

(D) It will never pass inspection

(19) By the rivers of Babylon we sat and wept when we remembered Zion. There on the poplars we hung our:

(A) Hammocks and lived in misery for seventy years

(B) Tools, determined to do no work for our enemies

(C) Harps, for there our captors asked us for songs

(D) Heads and prayed that God would soon return us to our homeland

(20) Search me, O God, and know my heart; test me and know my anxious thoughts.

(A) Forgive the iniquity you find in my life

(B) See if there is any offensive way in me, and lead me in the way everlasting

(C) Judge me not, for I am weak and weary

(D) Grant me your everlasting peace and help me live for you

May I Have Your Attention, Please?

As you read through the Bible, you find many different ways that God made his presence known. Some of the methods were unique, onetime phenomena. Others, such as dreams and angels, were used numerous times with various people, although only one instance has been selected for the purposes of this exercise. Match each person (or group of persons) listed below with the innovative way God communicated to either inform or confirm what he wanted the appropriate person to do. (Note: You may find more than one correct answer for a few of the methods listed.)

God's Method of Communication

(1) A talking (and quite intelligent) donkey

(2) A bush on fire that did not burn up

(3) People suddenly started speaking in different languages and couldn't communicate with anyone else

(4) People suddenly started speaking in different languages and could communicate with *everyone* else

(5) Loss of the ability to speak

(6) A voice in the night (four times)

(7) A gentle whisper (following a great wind, an earthquake, and a fire)

(8) Use of the Urim and Thummim (two sacred lots, perhaps stones, that were located on the breastplate of the high priest)

(9) Casting lots

(10) A pillar of cloud and a pillar of fire

(11) Writing on a wall

(12) A blinding light and voice on the road to Damascus

(13) Angels who literally dragged people out of a dangerous situation

(14) A wet fleece on dry ground, and then a dry fleece atop wet, dewy ground

(15) Sound effects (the sound of marching in the tops of the trees)

(16) A dream of angels ascending and descending a staircase (ladder)

(17) A visit in a fiery furnace

(18) Overnight, the person's staff budded, blossomed, and produced almonds

(19) A prophet with a personal message (in this case, Elijah predicting a multiyear drought)

(20) The shadow of the sun reversed itself and moved backward along ten steps on a stairway

Communicator

(A) Aaron
(B) Ahab (A king of Israel)
(C) Balaam
(D) Belshazzar (A Babylonian king)
(E) David
(F) Disciples in the early church
(G) Elijah
(H) Gideon
(I) Hezekiah (A king of Judah)
(J) Israelites in the wilderness
(K) Jacob
(L) Joshua
(M) Lot and his family
(N) Moses
(O) Paul
(P) People building the Tower of Babel
(Q) Sailors on Jonah's getaway ship
(R) Samuel
(S) Shadrach, Meshach, and Abednego
(T) Zechariah (or Zacharias) (The father of John the Baptist)

8

Complete the Proverb

The book of Proverbs was written by a number of knowledgeable contributors, including Solomon, the wisest person who has ever lived. So here's a chance to see how wise *you* are. Below are the beginnings of twenty proverbs. See if you can choose the correct ending for each one.

(1) The fear of the LORD is:
(A) A path to righteousness
(B) The beginning of knowledge
(C) A result of the guilt of sinners
(D) Avoided by those who love him

(2) Trust in the LORD with all your heart and lean not on your own understanding; in all your ways acknowledge him, and:
(A) He will make your paths straight
(B) You will discover success and honor
(C) You will never find need to weep
(D) He will anoint you with power

(3) Can a man scoop fire into his lap without his clothes being burned? Can a man walk on hot coals without his feet being scorched? So is he who:

(A) Seeks dishonest gain, for he will never find contentment

(B) Allows his anger to get out of control; he knows not peace of mind

(C) Sleeps with another man's wife; no one who touches her will go unpunished

(D) Seeks wisdom through divination and occult practices; his future is ruin

(4) As vinegar to the teeth and smoke to the eyes, so is:

(A) The scent of an immoral woman

(B) The behavior of a rich and thoughtless man

(C) A sluggard to those who send him

(D) The advice of a fool

(5) Like a gold ring in a pig's snout is:

(A) A king with no respect for his people

(B) A judge who takes bribes

(C) He who thinks too highly of himself

(D) A beautiful woman who shows no discretion

(6) A wife of noble character is her husband's crown, but a disgraceful wife:

(A) Is his dunce cap

(B) Is like decay in his bones

(C) Must seek wisdom and honor

(D) Brings him only shame

(7) The way of a fool seems right to him, but a wise man:

(A) Isn't afraid to ask for directions

(B) Heeds only the Word of the LORD

(C) Listens to advice

(D) Is hard to find

(8) Diligent hands will rule, but:

(A) Idle hands are the devil's workshop

(B) Laziness ends in slave labor

(C) Sloth is a deadly sin

(D) All work and no play makes Solomon a dull boy

(9) He who spares the rod hates his son, but he who loves him:

(A) Needs not the rod at all

(B) Is quick to punish him

(C) Is careful to discipline him

(D) Picks up the rod and takes him fishing

(10) There is a way that seems right to a man, but:

(A) A woman quickly shows him why it is wrong

(B) He still loves to pursue folly

(C) It is the LORD's way that matters

(D) In the end it leads to death

(11) A heart at peace gives life to the body, but:

(A) Is as rare as a precious jewel

(B) Trouble is a snare that destroys contentment

(C) Men who rage against God are without hope

(D) Envy rots the bones

(12) A gentle answer turns away wrath, but:
(A) A harsh word stirs up anger
(B) A firm word is heard in the heat of an argument
(C) A kind word gains an even better response
(D) Sometimes the other person just needs a good kick in the seat of the pants

(13) Pride goes before destruction:
(A) As sloth goes before poverty
(B) And temptation goes before pride
(C) A haughty spirit before a fall
(D) The arrogant man will be laid low

(14) Better to meet a bear robbed of her cubs than:
(A) A woman scorned
(B) A fool in his folly
(C) A disobedient and rebellious child
(D) A used-cart salesman who won't take no for an answer

(15) Better to live on a corner of the roof than:
(A) In a home bought with dishonest gain
(B) In a field marked with the damages of war
(C) Work for an unrighteous master
(D) Share a house with a quarrelsome wife

(16) Train a child in the way he should go:
(A) And then you'll need to remind him a dozen times every day
(B) Yet he will seek his own path
(C) And when he is old he will not turn from it
(D) And do not despair when he strays from it

(17) An honest answer is:

(A) Likely to be rejected

(B) Like newfound treasure

(C) Like the brightest star in the canopy of the heavens

(D) Like a kiss on the lips

(18) If your enemy is hungry, give him food to eat; if he is thirsty, give him water to drink. In doing this, you will:

(A) Honor the LORD your God

(B) Help him see the error of his ways

(C) Henceforth have a friend

(D) Heap burning coals on his head

(19) If a man loudly blesses his neighbor early in the morning:

(A) It will be taken as a curse

(B) The glory of the LORD will fill the village

(C) He will prosper the whole day long

(D) His conscience is clear before God

(20) As iron sharpens iron:

(A) So one man sharpens another

(B) The soldier prepares for war

(C) The gleam of the metal is the pride of the blacksmith

(D) God's law sharpens the mind of a man

9

Dreams and Visions

In the Bible, God communicated to numerous people through dreams and visions: both believers and nonbelievers, in the Old Testament and New Testament. Below are just a few of the fascinating visions and dreams of Bible characters. Match the dream and/or vision with the appropriate person (listed at the end of the chapter).

Dream and/or Vision

(1) Dreamed of Jesus' innocence but was unable to sway a spouse who had the authority to prevent his crucifixion

(2) Dreamed that the sun, moon, and eleven stars (representing his family) were bowing down to him

(3) Had a vision of angels surrounding God's throne and was greatly upset at his "unclean" state until an angel touched his lips with a live coal

(4) One of his five books of the Bible is almost entirely the account of a vision he had of the last days, including a beast (the antichrist), Armageddon, a scroll with seven seals, and the four horsemen of the apocalypse

(5) Dreamed of a stairway to heaven, with angels ascending and descending

(6) Though his book is better known for other stories (such as a fiery furnace and lions' den), this prophet also recorded dreams and visions of assorted beasts, future kingdoms, seventy "sevens," God as the "Ancient of Days," and more

(7) As confirmation that he would indeed have many descendants who would possess much land, this person had a conversation with God in a vision and saw a smoking firepot and torch pass between an array of recently slaughtered animals

(8) Had a vision of a man begging, "Come over to Macedonia and help us"

(9) After being among the first to encounter Jesus, had a dream to return home a different way for safety's sake

(10) Dreamed of three baskets of bread on his head being eaten by birds (which turned out to mean that he would die three days later)

(11) Had a vision of heavenly creatures moving on what appeared to be "made like a wheel intersecting a wheel"; the final nine chapters of his book describe his vision of a temple, those who serve in it, its furnishings, and its surroundings

(12) Dreamed of a great statue with head of gold, chest and arms of silver, belly and thighs of bronze, legs of iron, and feet of iron mixed with baked clay; a rock struck and demolished the feet of the statue, then the rock then became a mountain (a foretelling of the kingdom of God that would ultimately topple human kingdoms and last forever)

(13) Told by God in a dream to "ask for whatever you want me to give you" (He asked for wisdom)

(14) An angel warned him in a dream to flee to Egypt, which saved the life of the baby Jesus

(15) Dreamed that seven ugly, skinny cows ate seven sleek, fat cows (signifying a coming famine)

(16) Had a vision where God told him to minister to Saul (Paul), even though at the time Paul had been trying to arrest all believers

(17) After his first vision, this youngster had to tell his mentor some distressing news about the man's family

(18) Had a vision of a large sheet lowered from heaven, containing both clean and unclean animals, and was instructed to "kill and eat" (The vision would later be understood as God's inclusion of Gentiles into the early church)

Dreamer

(A) Abraham

(B) Ananias

(C) Daniel

(D) Ezekiel

(E) Isaiah

(F) Jacob

(G) John

(H) Joseph (the coat-of-many-colors guy from the Old Testament)

(I) Joseph (the husband of Mary in the New Testament)

(J) Nebuchadnezzar, king of Babylon

(K) Paul

(L) Peter

(M) Pharaoh

(N) Pharaoh's baker

(O) Pilate's wife

(P) Samuel

(Q) Solomon

(R) Wise Men (Magi)

10

The Writing Prophets

Many prophets are referenced in the Bible, but sixteen of them have books bearing their names. When we pick up the Bible for a little inspirational reading, many of us avoid the prophetic books—which comprise a hefty amount of the Old Testament. Yet you might know a little more about the four major (Isaiah, Jeremiah, Ezekiel, and Daniel) and twelve minor prophets than you realize. See how you do at matching the clues below with the prophets listed at the end of the chapter.

Distinctive Fact or Accomplishment

(1) Had much to say about "the day of the LORD" when God's judgment would be felt by sinful nations (He probably had to sit in the back at prophet school if they were seated alphabetically)

(2) Not only had a close encounter with some large felines, but also saw some incredible visions that figure into numerous interpretations of end-times events

(3) Although the people of Nineveh repented after Jonah's visit, they soon reverted to wickedness and this prophet correctly predicted their eventual downfall

(4) When the wise men stopped by Jerusalem seeking the Christ child, Herod's scholars consulted this prophet's writing to determine that the Messiah was to be born in Bethlehem

(5) He is often referred to as "the weeping prophet" because he got little respect or positive response as he tried to prepare his people for a coming seventy-year exile; among other things, his writings were burned, he was imprisoned, and he spent some time in a miry mud pit; he is also credited with writing the book of Lamentations

(6) His eventual reconciliation with his promiscuous wife was a symbol of God's ongoing love and commitment even after Israel had deserted the Lord

(7) "Will a man rob God?" this prophet asked his tightfisted people; he also predicted the coming of "the prophet Elijah before that great and dreadful day of the LORD comes," and he provided the final word of the Old Testament: "curse"

(8) This major prophet was more involved than most when it came to being a personal example of God's messages (for example, when his wife died he was not allowed to mourn publicly because the temple was about to be destroyed and the exiled people would not be allowed to linger and grieve);

one of his best-known visions took place in a valley of dry bones and, according to an old spiritual, he "saw the wheel."

(9) He wrote the shortest of the Old Testament books of prophecy

(10) A priest as well as a prophet, his book records a number of spectacular visions including a flying scroll, four chariots, and a woman in a basket; it concludes with the Lord standing on the Mount of Olives, splitting it in half

(11) One of his prophecies was recalled immediately after the Holy Spirit first came to the believers of the early church

(12) When the Jewish exiles were finally allowed to return from Babylon to their homeland, this prophet was there to exhort them to rebuild the temple that had been destroyed

(13) This prophet, a shepherd and tender of sycamore fig trees who was called to prophesy to Israel, was a big proponent of social justice (He probably sat in the front at prophet school)

(14) This major prophet is mentioned by name twenty-two times in the New Testament—more than any other; one time in the synagogue at Nazareth, Jesus read from this guy's book and announced: "Today this scripture is fulfilled in your hearing"

(15) Unlike the other prophetic writings, this prophet's book is more like a question-and-answer conversation between himself and God

(16) He resisted going to the capital of Assyria until a well-known incident with a fish; he later had a lesser-known encounter with a worm

Prophet Described

(A) Isaiah
(B) Jeremiah
(C) Ezekiel
(D) Daniel
(E) Hosea
(F) Joel
(G) Amos
(H) Obadiah
(I) Jonah
(J) Micah
(K) Nahum
(L) Habakkuk
(M) Zephaniah
(N) Haggai
(O) Zechariah
(P) Malachi

11

Sixteen Horrible Deaths

We've all got to go sometime. [Actually, there are a couple of biblical exceptions: Enoch (Genesis 5:23–24; Hebrews 11:5) and Elijah (2 Kings 2:11–12). But most of us tend to die after we've lived our lives.] Still, some deaths stand out a bit more than others. See if you can match these graphic deaths with the biblical characters listed at the end of the chapter.

Circumstances of Death

(1) Head hammered to ground with a tent peg

(2) The earth "opened its mouth" and they went down alive into the grave

(3) The Lord's anger burned against him and he fell down dead after touching the ark of the covenant, even though he was trying to keep it from falling

(4) Mauled by two bears after insulting the prophet Elisha

(5) Had an assistant quickly kill him after a woman dropped a millstone from a tower and cracked his head

(6) Ehud (a judge) plunged a sword into his belly and his belly fat closed over it

(7) After being beheaded, the head was served on a platter at the request of an impressive dancer

(8) Hanged on a gallows he built specifically to execute someone else

(9) Thrown from a window by eunuchs and trampled underfoot by horses; all that was recovered were skull, feet, and hands

(10) While hanging by hair from an oak tree, had three javelins plunged into heart and was finished off by ten soldiers

(11) Butt of a spear was thrust into his stomach so hard it came out his back

(12) Heard the ark of the covenant had been captured, fell backward off chair, broke neck, and died

(13) Didn't correct crowd when they called him a god, so an angel of the Lord struck him down and he was eaten by worms

(14) In spite of attempts to remain incognito during battle, was killed when "someone drew his bow at random" and the arrow hit him between the sections of his armor

(15) Lied about a gift given to the church, and fell dead as a result

(16) Either during or after hanging himself, "he fell headlong, his body burst open and all his intestines spilled out"

Victim

(A) Forty-two young men
(B) Abimelech (A rogue judge)
(C) Absalom (Son of King David)
(D) Ahab
(E) Ananias and Sapphira
(F) Asahel (A brother of Joab, David's commander)
(G) Eglon, king of Moab
(H) Eli (A priest)
(I) Haman
(J) King Herod
(K) Jezebel
(L) John the Baptist
(M) Judas Iscariot
(N) Korah and his followers
(O) Sisera (A cruel commander of an enemy army)
(P) Uzzah

The Original Christmas Story

Judging from lawn decorations in early December, some might assume that the first Christmas involved the baby Jesus in a manger surrounded by shepherds, wise men, little drummer boys, red-nosed reindeer, frosty snowmen, and numerous other characters. Yet of everything in the Bible, the one thing most of us know is the Christmas story . . . or do we? Answer the following questions and find out. You may be surprised how many—or how few—of our Christmas traditions are actually based on what's found in the Bible.

(1) The Jewish people were looking for the Messiah to come, but first they were to expect:

(A) A world of hurt because of their sins

(B) The prophet Elijah

(C) A great flock of angels with big news

(D) A sign among the heavens

(2) According to the prophet Micah, Jesus was to be born:

(A) In a miraculous way

(B) Out of wedlock

(C) In Bethlehem
(D) Under a bad sign

**(3) The angel who told Mary to prepare for Jesus'
birth was:**
(A) Gabriel
(B) Michael
(C) John
(D) Denzel

**(4) When Zechariah (the father of John the Baptist)
questioned this same angel in the temple, God made him:**
(A) Deaf
(B) Blind
(C) Dumb
(D) Lunch

**(5) Zechariah doubted the angel's message that his wife,
Elizabeth, would have a child because they both were:**
(A) Sad and full of tears
(B) Scared and full of fears
(C) Young and full of beers
(D) Old and full of years

**(6) When Mary discovered she was pregnant, she and
Joseph were:**
(A) Already married
(B) About to become engaged
(C) Pledged to be married
(D) Only hookin' up

(7) Joseph didn't take the news of Mary's pregnancy too well. He wanted to:

(A) Stone her

(B) Kill himself

(C) Publicly humiliate her

(D) Get a quickie divorce

(8) The baby was named Jesus ("the Lord saves") in response to whom/what?

(A) Gabriel

(B) Mary

(C) Joseph

(D) *1001 Hebrew Baby Names*

(9) Mary and Joseph were in Bethlehem rather than Nazareth because of:

(A) A famine

(B) Caesar Augustus

(C) A warning from an angel

(D) Some really, really bad directions

(10) Which of the following is the only correct statement based on the information provided in the Bible?

(A) Jesus was born in an inn

(B) Jesus was born in a stable

(C) Jesus was born among the sheep and cattle

(D) After Jesus was born, he was placed in a manger

(11) The shepherds first heard the news from:

(A) A single angel

(B) A multitude of the heavenly host

(C) The wise men

(D) Fellow shepherds

(12) The shepherds were told to look for what sign?

(A) A special star in the heavens

(B) A baby wrapped in cloths and lying in a manger

(C) A large gathering outside a stable

(D) A fish symbol on the back of a donkey

(13) Which of the following are the only persons you *will* find in the biblical story of the birth of Jesus?

(A) Three kings

(B) An innkeeper and his wife

(C) Terrified shepherds

(D) A choir of singing angels

(14) How did the wise men (Magi) find Jesus?

(A) They followed a star directly to where he was

(B) They followed a star to Jerusalem, where they received additional directions to Bethlehem

(C) They bumped into the shepherds, who pointed the way

(D) They were wise men—they just knew where to look

(15) When the wise men found Jesus, he was in a:

(A) Manger

(B) Stable

(C) Bassinette

(D) House

(16) The Bible tells of _____ wise men who presented _____ gifts to the baby Jesus.

(A) Three . . . three

(B) Three . . . an unspecified number of

(C) An unspecified number of . . . an unspecified number of

(D) An unspecified number of . . . three

(17) When the wise men didn't return to Herod as he had asked, Herod:

(A) Sent soldiers to retrieve them

(B) Went to look for Jesus himself

(C) Gave orders to kill all newborns

(D) Ordered that all male children under two be killed

(18) When Jesus was first presented in the temple, who recognized him as someone who would be very special?

(A) A man waiting to see the Christ before he died, and a very old widow

(B) A little child

(C) The high priest

(D) A number of religious leaders

(19) Before Mary, Joseph, and Jesus went from Bethlehem to Nazareth, they had to:

(A) Ensure that the wise men had arrived home safely

(B) Flee for their lives and hang out in another country for a while

(C) Baptize Jesus

(D) Register Jesus in the census

(20) How did Mary respond to all of the events of Jesus' birth?

(A) She was "sore afraid"

(B) She asked God a lot of questions

(C) She "treasured up all these things and pondered them in her heart"

(D) She sent clever, informative Christmas letters out to all her friends

13

The Life of Jesus

No short book can adequately cover the life and ministry of Jesus. But the following true/false quiz provides a brief sampling of the content of the Gospels: Matthew, Mark, Luke, and John.

(1) Even when Jesus was twelve years old, everyone who heard him discussing spiritual matters with religious leaders was amazed at his understanding and answers.

(2) Jesus was about twenty-five when he began his ministry.

(3) When Jesus was baptized by John the Baptist, he heard the voice of God from heaven and the Holy Spirit descended like a dove and rested on him.

(4) When Jesus was tempted in the wilderness, he had just fasted for forty days and forty nights.

(5) Jesus withstood each of three temptations simply by quoting a verse from the Scriptures (what we know as the Old Testament).

(6) When Jesus called Andrew and Peter to be his disciples, they were fishing in the Dead Sea.

(7) Jesus spent an entire night in prayer just prior to choosing the twelve apostles.

(8) One time Jesus picked up a stick and started driving animals and money changers out of the temple.

(9) Jesus raised three people (that we know of) from the dead.

(10) When Jesus said, "I have not found anyone in Israel with such great faith," he was talking about a Roman centurion.

(11) Jesus not only walked on water, he also calmed a terrible storm just by speaking to it.

(12) After designating twelve apostles, Jesus later sent out seventy-two disciples in pairs into towns he planned to visit.

(13) Although most of the religious leaders opposed Jesus, a Pharisee named Zacchaeus met with him at night to discuss spiritual things.

(14) At a well, Jesus had an interesting discussion with a Samaritan woman who had had five husbands and was currently living with yet another guy.

(15) Although Jesus met with opposition in a lot of places, he was warmly received in his hometown of Nazareth.

(16) Jesus lived in Nazareth his entire adult life.

(17) It is safe to presume that Peter was married because Jesus healed his mother-in-law.

(18) Jesus nicknamed James and John (the sons of Zebedee) "Boanerges," which meant "sons of lightning."

(19) Jesus was known as a glutton and a drunkard as well as a friend of tax collectors and sinners.

(20) The ministry of Jesus and the disciples was supported financially by a group of women who had been cured of evil spirits and diseases.

(21) One time Jesus cast out a number of demons from a man, and they immediately inhabited a herd of about two thousand sheep that then ran down a hill into a lake and drowned.

(22) A woman was healed of a bleeding disease that had lasted twelve years just by touching the edge of Jesus' cloak.

THE LIFE OF JESUS

(23) One time Jesus fed a crowd of five thousand men (plus women and children) using only five loaves of bread and two fish; later he performed a similar feat for a crowd of four thousand men (plus women and children).

(24) Once when a non-Jewish woman asked Jesus to heal her daughter, Jesus told the woman: "I was sent only to the lost sheep of Israel. . . . It is not right to take the children's bread and toss it to their dogs."

(25) Three of Jesus' disciples witnessed his transfiguration when his face shone like the sun, his clothes became as white as a flash of light, and he conversed with Moses and Elijah.

(26) After Jesus raised Lazarus from the dead, the religious leaders not only wanted to kill Jesus, but they plotted to kill Lazarus as well.

(27) One time Jesus healed ten lepers and expressed disappointment when only half of them came back to thank him.

(28) At times Jesus had to break up arguments among the disciples about which of them was the greatest and even had to deal with the mother of a couple of them who requested special favor for her sons.

(29) One time Jesus cursed an olive tree because it wasn't bearing fruit, and by the next day it had withered and died.

(30) At the Last Supper, Jesus washed all the disciples' feet, although Judas resisted.

14

The Teachings of Jesus

The Bible tells us that when Jesus spoke, "the crowds were amazed ... because he taught as one who had authority, and not as their teachers of the law" (Matthew 7:28–29). Below are a few statements concerning his teachings. See if you can identify which ones are true and which ones aren't entirely correct.

(1) When Jesus started preaching, he echoed the message of John the Baptist: "Repent, for the kingdom of heaven is near."

(2) In the Beatitudes (the prelude to the Sermon on the Mount), Jesus said the meek were "blessed" because someday they would see justice done.

(3) Jesus said his followers could not enter the kingdom of heaven unless their righteousness exceeded that of the teachers of the law and the Pharisees.

(4) In the Sermon on the Mount, Jesus compared his followers to salt, light, and a city on a hill.

(5) Jesus said he had come to do away with the outdated Law and (writings of) the Prophets.

(6) In matters such as murder, adultery, and divorce, Jesus promoted narrower, more restrictive guidelines than what were being taught at the time.

(7) The Lord's Prayer is included in Jesus' Sermon on the Mount.

(8) The Golden Rule ("Do to others what you would have them do to you") is part of Jesus' Sermon on the Mount.

(9) Jesus told parables to clarify the mystery of the kingdom of God for everyone.

(10) Jesus reminded his listeners that the gate to heaven is wide and easy to find.

(11) Jesus told about forty parables, including one praising a dishonest business manager and one comparing God to an unjust judge who granted a request just to get a persistent widow off his back.

(12) Jesus lost a lot of followers when he started talking about people "eat[ing] my flesh and drink[ing] my blood."

(13) Jesus taught that the greatest in the kingdom of heaven would be those people who worked hard and remained most faithful to God.

(14) Jesus' parable of the good Samaritan was preceded by a question ("And who is my neighbor?") and concludes with a challenge: "Go and do likewise."

(15) Jesus taught that considering becoming one of his disciples required planning and forethought in much the same way that a building project or military campaign would.

(16) Jesus' parable of the prodigal son concludes with a joyful reunion of the father and his two sons.

(17) Jesus taught that if the Law and Prophets weren't enough to persuade a person to repent, he or she wouldn't be convinced even if someone were to come back from the dead with a personal message.

(18) Jesus said that the entire Old Testament (the Law and the Prophets) was summed up in two commandments: "Love the Lord your God with all your heart and with all your soul and with all your mind and with all your strength," and "Love your neighbor as yourself."

(19) Jesus promised to return to earth after his death, but said that only a few people would be able to discern the day and the hour of his return.

(20) Jesus told his disciples that anyone who had seen him had seen God the Father.

Jesus' Death and Resurrection

With the Gospels' four different eyewitness accounts of Jesus' death, we have a wealth of information to draw from. Some writers recorded certain facts, and other writers focused on different things. But they all agree that while the death of Jesus was horrid and brutal, his resurrection was glorious and certain. The following questions cover just a few of the events of the last days of Jesus on earth.

(1) Which Old Testament prophet foretold a Messiah who would be "pierced for our transgressions," "led like a lamb to the slaughter," "assigned a grave with the wicked" and would "[pour] out his life unto death, and [be] numbered with the transgressors"?

(A) Isaiah

(B) Jeremiah

(C) Ezekiel

(D) Obadiah

(2) Many of the religious leaders had long wanted to silence Jesus, but they were afraid to do it during Passover because:

(A) It would have interfered with their family seders

(B) It was against their law to hold an execution during a religious holiday

(C) They were afraid the people might riot if they tried to harm Jesus

(D) They wanted his death to look like an accident

(3) Where did Jesus and the disciples eat the Last Supper?

(A) In the banquet hall of an inn

(B) At the temple

(C) At the home of Mary Magdalene

(D) In the upper room of a stranger's house

(4) At his Last Supper, Jesus identified Judas Iscariot as the one who would betray him by:

(A) Handing him a piece of bread

(B) Proclaiming, "You are the man!"

(C) Kissing him

(D) Washing his feet

(5) After the Last Supper, Jesus took Peter, James, and John with him to pray in the Garden of Gethsemane, but they kept:

(A) Discussing the meal

(B) Wandering off

(C) Arguing among themselves

(D) Falling asleep

(6) When the religious leaders arrived with Judas, Judas kissed Jesus and said:

(A) "This is the man"

(B) "What I do, I do for your own good"

(C) "Greetings, Rabbi!"

(D) "Seize him!"

(7) Before the disciples all ran away and deserted Jesus, Peter first:

(A) Whipped out a sword and wounded one of those present

(B) Began to weep

(C) Expressed his great faith in Jesus

(D) Tried to reason with the religious leaders

(8) What was the official charge against Jesus?

(A) Healing on the Sabbath

(B) Blasphemy

(C) Heresy

(D) Idolatry

(9) During Jesus' various trials that evening, which of the following officials did he _not_ appear before?

(A) Annas and Caiaphas (Jewish high priests)

(B) Pontius Pilate (the Roman procurator)

(C) Caesar Augustus (the Roman Emperor)

(D) Herod Antipas (the Roman-appointed ruler of Galilee)

(10) Less than a week before his crucifixion, Jesus had entered Jerusalem triumphantly, riding on a:
(A) Chariot
(B) White stallion
(C) Mule
(D) Donkey

(11) Pilate first attempted to appease the crowd without having to kill Jesus, but what finally changed his mind?
(A) Jesus insulted him
(B) The crowd threatened to claim he was disloyal to Caesar
(C) The crowd literally dragged Jesus away
(D) He had scheduled a meeting with Herod and had to make a quick decision

(12) What may have been one reason Pilate was reluctant to have Jesus put to death?
(A) His wife had had a dream of Jesus' innocence
(B) He had been impressed during a previous meeting with Jesus in the middle of the night
(C) Jesus had healed him
(D) Pilate and Jesus were distant relatives

(13) Jesus was flogged, stripped, mocked, dressed in a scarlet robe and "crown" of thorns, spat on, repeatedly beaten on the head with his "staff," then crucified between two:
(A) Religious zealots
(B) Murderers
(C) Robbers
(D) Soldiers who had deserted their posts

(14) Pilate had a sign placed on Jesus' cross which said, in three languages:
(A) "Jesus of Nazareth, the king of the Jews"
(B) "This man claimed to be the king of the Jews"
(C) "Behold what happens to enemies of Rome!"
(D) "I find no fault with this man"

(15) From the cross, Jesus spoke to:
(A) Simon Peter
(B) His mother, his Father, a new believer in him, and John
(C) Mary Magdalene
(D) The soldiers who were mocking him

(16) One of Jesus' statements from the cross was a portion of a:
(A) Psalm
(B) Proverb
(C) Lamentation
(D) Prayer of Moses

(17) Which of the following events did *not* take place immediately after Jesus died?
(A) The curtain in the temple was torn in two, from top to bottom
(B) The earth shook and rocks split
(C) Tombs came open and many dead people came back to life
(D) The criminals crucified on both sides of him repented

(18) Where was Jesus buried?
(A) In a "potter's field" (poor man's cemetery) purchased with the money Judas had received to betray him
(B) In a tomb intended for a family member
(C) In a tomb intended for one of the disciples
(D) In a tomb intended for a rich and prominent Jewish religious leader

(19) The people who anointed Jesus' body were:
(A) Nicodemus and Joseph of Arimathea
(B) A group of women
(C) The disciples
(D) Unknown because the Bible doesn't say

(20) Jesus was crucified at a place called Golgotha (or Calvary), which means:
(A) Execution Hill
(B) Place of the Skull
(C) Hill of Pain
(D) Beautiful Overlook

(21) Jesus' resurrection was first announced by:
(A) A thundering voice from heaven
(B) The disciples
(C) Two angels at the tomb
(D) The risen Jesus himself

(22) The first to hear of Jesus' resurrection were:
(A) Mary Magdalene and some other women
(B) The disciples

(C) The guards at the tomb

(D) A group of believers in an upper room

(23) The first person to encounter the risen Jesus was:

(A) Simon Peter

(B) Mary, Jesus' mother

(C) Mary Magdalene

(D) John

(24) What did Jesus do to prove he wasn't a ghost?

(A) He let the disciples examine his hands and feet, and he ate a piece of fish

(B) He opened a door and walked into the room

(C) He ate bread and drank wine

(D) He embraced each of the eleven disciples

(25) How much time passed between Jesus' resurrection and his ascension into heaven?

(A) Three days

(B) One week

(C) Two weeks

(D) Forty days

16

A Baker's Dozen of Disciples

The New Testament makes numerous references to Jesus' disciples (or apostles) as a group. But as individuals, some of them get considerably more coverage than the others. See if you can match the clues to the thirteen disciples (listed at the end of the chapter). Why thirteen? You'll find out as you start matching.

Clues

(1) Was willing to die with Jesus, yet didn't believe in the resurrection at first because he had been absent when Jesus appeared

(2) Walked on water, but three times denied knowing Jesus

(3) Initially a disciple of John the Baptist who left to follow Jesus and immediately recruited his brother, Simon (Peter)

(4) Along with his brother John, was given the name Boanerges ("sons of thunder") by Jesus, and was the first of the Twelve to be put to death

(5) Always referred to himself as "the disciple whom Jesus loved"

(6) Once asked Jesus to "show us the Father." Another time was responsible for helping some Gentiles who wanted to meet with Jesus (Perhaps they asked him because of his Greek-sounding name)

(7) Though he was skeptical when told about Jesus, at their first meeting Jesus called him, "A true Israelite, in whom there is nothing false"

(8) Was collecting taxes when Jesus called him

(9) His name is often followed by "the Little" or "the Younger" to differentiate him from another disciple with the same name

(10) He may have belonged to a radical political party opposed to Roman control of his country

(11) Nothing significant is known of him, but he is called Thaddaeus in a couple of places (and if you had his name today, you might prefer a different one as well)

(12) The treasurer for the disciples . . . and probably not a wise choice

(13) Chosen by casting lots to replace Judas Iscariot (after his suicide) as one of the apostles

Disciple Described

(A) Andrew
(B) James, son of Zebedee
(C) James, son of Alphaeus
(D) John
(E) Judas Iscariot
(F) Judas, son of James
(G) Matthew (Levi)
(H) Matthias
(I) Nathanael (Bartholomew)
(J) Philip
(K) Simon Peter
(L) Simon the Zealot
(M) Thomas

17

Sound Bytes

The Bible doesn't just tell stories. Many times it records the conversations and statements of its characters, not unlike the highlights of a nightly newscast. See if you can match each of the following sound bytes with the appropriate speaker (listed at the end of the chapter).

Biblical Quote

(1) "How will this be, since I am a virgin?"

(2) "Curse God and die!"

(3) "Listen, you rebels, must we bring you water out of this rock?"

(4) "Where you go I will go, and where you stay I will stay. Your people will be my people and your God my God."

(5) "You are the Christ, the Son of the living God."

(6) "And spare my people—this is my request. For I and my people have been sold for destruction and slaughter and annihilation."

(7) "Look, I see heaven open and the Son of Man standing at the right hand of God."

(8) "Among you stands one you do not know. He is the one who comes after me, the thongs of whose sandals I am not worthy to untie."

(9) "Jerusalem lies in ruins, and its gates have been burned with fire. Come, let us rebuild the wall of Jerusalem, and we will no longer be in disgrace."

(10) "Unless I see the nail marks in his hands and put my finger where the nails were, and put my hand into his side, I will not believe it."

(11) "I know that my Redeemer lives, and that in the end he will stand upon the earth."

(12) "Surely he was the Son of God!"

(13) "Choose for yourselves this day whom you will serve. . . . But as for me and my household, we will serve the LORD."

(14) "You are the man!"

(15) "You have been unfaithful; you have married foreign women. . . . Separate yourselves from the peoples around you and from your foreign wives."

(16) "Do you understand what you are reading?"

(17) "Look, Lord! Here and now I give half of my possessions to the poor, and if I have cheated anybody out of anything, I will pay back four times the amount."

(18) "Pick me up and throw me into the sea, and it will become calm."

(19) "My master has withheld nothing from me except you, because you are his wife. How then could I do such a wicked thing and sin against God?"

(20) "How can a man be born when he is old? Surely he cannot enter a second time into his mother's womb to be born!"

(21) "Here am I. Send me!"

(22) "The LORD who delivered me from the paw of the lion and the paw of the bear will deliver me from the hand of this Philistine."

(23) "Give me here on a platter the head of John the Baptist."

(24) "Shall I crucify your king?"

(25) "Please test your servants for ten days: Give us nothing but vegetables to eat and water to drink. Then compare our appearance with that of the young men who eat the royal food."

Speaker

(A) Centurion at Jesus' crucifixion
(B) Daniel
(C) Daughter of Herodias (Probably Salome)
(D) David
(E) Esther
(F) Ezra
(G) Isaiah
(H) Job

(I) Job's wife
(J) John the Baptist
(K) Jonah
(L) Joseph (The one in the Old Testament)
(M) Joshua
(N) Mary
(O) Moses
(P) Nathan
(Q) Nehemiah
(R) Nicodemus
(S) Philip (The deacon, not the apostle)
(T) Pontius Pilate
(U) Ruth
(V) Simon Peter
(W) Stephen (A leader of the early church)
(X) Thomas
(Y) Zacchaeus

The Life of Paul

Next to Jesus, Paul is probably the most prominent person in the New Testament. We discover much about his fascinating life in the last half of the book of Acts, and other helpful clues are found throughout his letters as well. See how much you know about Paul with the following exercise. Since it's in true-or-false format, you'll have a fifty-fifty chance of getting correct answers even on those you don't know!

(1) Paul was originally named Saul, but God changed his name to Paul.

(2) The first time we see Paul in the Bible, he is tending to the clothes of a crowd of men stoning a believer to death.

(3) Paul was born in Tarsus, a capital city known for its intellectual atmosphere and civic pride.

(4) Of the twenty-seven books in the New Testament, Paul is credited with writing thirteen of them.

(5) Paul was a Roman citizen.

(6) Paul received essentially all of his religious training after he had a dramatic conversion to Christianity.

(7) Paul's conversion took place while he was traveling from Damascus to Jerusalem.

(8) After Paul's initial encounter with Jesus, he was blind for three days.

(9) The believers were reluctant to trust Paul until God directed Peter to meet with him and welcome him into the church.

(10) Saul's conversion alarmed the Jewish religious leaders to the point that they staked out the city gates, planning to kill him, and Paul's new friends had to help him escape Damascus by lowering him down the wall in a basket.

(11) Paul went on a number of missionary journeys, telling people about Jesus and establishing churches, the first of which he traveled with a faithful disciple named Barnabas and a young believer named John Mark.

(12) A disagreement between Paul and Barnabas prevented them from taking additional trips together.

(13) At one of their stops, Paul and his companion were mistaken for the Greek gods Zeus and Hermes, and the people brought animals to sacrifice to them.

(14) On Paul's first journey, he was stoned by a hostile crowd and left for dead.

(15) Paul had hoped to return from his first journey in time to attend a council in Jerusalem but missed it due to the events of his trip.

(16) On his second journey, Paul cast a spirit out of a pesky slave girl in Philippi, which led to his being arrested, stripped, flogged, and jailed.

(17) An angel miraculously helped Paul escape prison in the middle of the night.

(18) In Athens, Paul found a good opportunity to tell others about Jesus when he came upon an altar with the inscription: "To an Unknown God."

(19) Paul never stayed more than a few months in one place before moving on to another.

(20) In one place, God worked through Paul so that hand-kerchiefs he had touched could be carried to sick people who would then be healed or released from an evil spirit.

(21) Paul ran into trouble in Ephesus when a religious revival threatened the business of a craftsmen's guild that made their income selling silver shrines of the goddess Hera.

(22) One time a young man fell asleep during one of Paul's sermons and died from a fall from a third-story window ledge, but Paul brought him back to life.

(23) A prophet used Paul's belt to warn him that he would run into trouble if he went to Jerusalem, but Paul went anyway.

(24) One time Paul caused suspicion because he was mistaken for an Egyptian terrorist.

(25) More than forty men took a solemn oath not to eat or drink anything until they had killed Paul.

(26) None of Paul's trials took very long. Each time he was arrested, he was released in a matter of days.

(27) At one point Paul might have been released, but he demanded a trial before Caesar, which necessitated a trip to Rome.

(28) Paul was once involved in a devastating shipwreck, but thanks to him no one died.

(29) Paul was bitten by a deadly viper, and when he didn't die as a result, the witnesses assumed he was a god.

(30) The book of Acts has a happy ending as Paul was declared not guilty and released to continue his ministry.

19

The Writings of Paul

When Paul wasn't on the road traveling, preaching, and establishing churches, he was frequently writing to comfort, advise, or encourage a person or church. Below are just a few of the things he wrote ... or then again, maybe he didn't. Can you tell Paul's genuine writings from the misstatements and inventions?

---

(1) In his writings, Paul occasionally expressed his own opinions along with inspired "comments from the Lord."

(2) Paul wrote that believers become not only God's children, but also his heirs—and coheirs with Jesus.

(3) In Paul's "love chapter" (1 Corinthians 13), he reminds us that knowledge, faith, and love will endure forever.

(4) Paul wrote of being imprisoned, flogged, beaten, stoned, shipwrecked (three times), adrift in the open sea for a night and a day, and numerous other sufferings.

(5) Paul calls his readers to be living sacrifices who conform to the world yet also are obedient to God.

(6) Paul described an "armor of God" for believers to wear that includes a belt of truth, shield of faith, and helmet of salvation, among other items.

(7) Paul referred to himself as the worst (or chief) of sinners.

(8) When Paul heard of a church member in a relationship with his father's wife (probably the man's stepmother), he advised that the church elders immediately meet with the man, pray with him, and restore him to fellowship.

(9) Paul tells believers to "pray continually."

(10) When Paul heard of two women involved in a public church disagreement, he called them by name in a letter, asking them to settle the matter.

(11) According to Paul, some people face temptations too powerful for anyone to endure, so other believers should remain alert and help see them through those situations.

(12) One time Paul wrote of a man who had been caught up into the seventh heaven where he heard inexpressible things he was not permitted to tell.

(13) Paul spoke in tongues.

(14) Paul assures us that we will have bodies in heaven, although they will be different from our earthly bodies.

(15) Paul compared the light of God in a believer's life to a treasure within a metal box.

(16) Paul says one good way to make sure others learn about Jesus is to become "yoked together" with unbelievers so that opportunities present themselves.

(17) Paul expressed a desire to be cursed and cut off from Christ if it would somehow help his fellow Jews to believe in Jesus.

(18) Satan gave Paul a "thorn in [his] flesh" that God would not remove, even though Paul pleaded three times.

(19) Paul considered himself "crucified with Christ."

(20) Paul defined the "fruit of the Spirit" as: "love, joy, peace, patience, kindness, goodness, faithfulness, gentleness and self-control."

(21) Paul tells believers that "each one should carry his own load" yet also acknowledges there are times when we should "carry each other's burdens."

(22) According to Paul, God's will is always going to be a mystery to us.

(23) When an outspoken group of agitators tried to demand circumcision for all believers, Paul wrote that he wished they would go the whole way and emasculate themselves.

(24) Paul said it's a good thing salvation comes by the grace of God because if it were based on good works, believers would tend to brag.

(25) Paul's letter to Philemon was primarily in regard to a runaway slave.

(26) Since God establishes all earthly authorities, Paul said, we are to submit to our governing bodies regardless of what we feel about them.

(27) Paul struggled to decide which he wanted more: to die or to continue to live.

(28) Paul said if unmarried people can't control themselves, it's better to marry than to burn with passion.

(29) Paul wrote Philippians, perhaps his most optimistic and joyful letter, while imprisoned.

(30) Paul recommended that when slaves became believers, their believing masters should set them free.

(31) Paul wrote that it is better to be wronged and cheated than for believers to file lawsuits against one another.

(32) Paul wrote that the anticipated return of Jesus is an event that should strike fear and terror in even the most faithful of believers.

(33) Paul says we should choose *not* to exercise certain spiritual freedoms in order to avoid creating a stumbling block for other believers who don't feel the same way.

(34) Paul assured Timothy, a young pastor, that the youngster's "spirit of timidity" was a gift from God.

(35) It is Paul's advice to make it a rule not to go to bed angry.

Where Do Babies Come From?

We may *think* we know where babies come from. But in the stories of the Bible, they come from letting husbands sleep with handmaids, from bartering for time with a mutual husband, from intense prayer, and from some far less noble methods. See what you know about the following biblical baby stories.

(1) After Cain killed Abel and was sentenced to wander the earth, leaving Eve without a child, she was "granted . . . another child in place of Abel" and named him:
(A) Enoch
(B) Seth
(C) Noah
(D) Howie

(2) When Sarah was unable to conceive and told Abraham to have a child with her handmaid, Hagar, what was the result?
(A) Hagar was also unable to have children
(B) They all lived together, happily ever after

(C) Hagar's baby created jealousy, and Sarah kicked them both out of the household

(D) Sarah became pregnant almost immediately

(3) After God told Rebekah, "Two nations are in your womb," what was unusual about the births of her twins, Jacob and Esau?

(A) They were conjoined

(B) They were identical, and no one could tell them apart

(C) The older one died almost immediately

(D) The younger one came out of the womb grasping the heel of the older one

(4) When Jacob's wives were competing to have children, what did Leah trade to her sister, Rachel, for the opportunity to sleep with their mutual husband?

(A) A new robe

(B) Mandrakes

(C) Five young lambs

(D) A time-share in the Dead Sea Saltwater Condominiums

(5) After Lot's daughters left Sodom and found themselves with no prospective husbands, they:

(A) Took vows of chastity

(B) Took turns getting their father drunk and sleeping with him

(C) Took their time until God provided them with husbands

(D) Took up occult practices in a desperate attempt to marry

(6) Prior to giving birth to Samuel, Hannah was childless and miserable, and she prayed so intently that a priest thought she was:
(A) Drunk
(B) Insane
(C) An angel
(D) Possessed

(7) What biblical figure was found as a baby and brought up as royalty yet was also raised by his own mother?
(A) Saul
(B) David
(C) Solomon
(D) Moses

(8) The prophet Hosea had an unfaithful wife and children (perhaps not his) whose names meant:
(A) "New Hope" and "Perseverance"
(B) "Why, Lord?" and "Second Chance"
(C) "Not Loved" and "Not My People"
(D) "Get Lost" and "Don't Come Back"

(9) Onan was a guy who tried to avoid providing children for his sister-in-law by:
(A) Never sleeping with her
(B) Killing their children as soon as they were born
(C) Spilling his semen on the ground
(D) Constantly standing close to the microwave

(10) Samson's parents were unable to have children until an angel told them to await his birth. And after spending time with each of them, the angel:

(A) Warned them not to speak of what they had seen and heard

(B) Shone with the radiance of the sun

(C) Ascended to heaven in the flame of a sacrificed goat

(D) Heard a bell ring and got his wings

(11) The father of John the Baptist doubted the angel-delivered news that his elderly wife would soon bear a son, and as a result he was:

(A) Unable to speak until John was born

(B) Immediately put to death

(C) Blinded for the rest of his life

(D) Temporarily stricken with leprosy

(12) Mary was chosen to give birth to Jesus because:

(A) She had found favor with God

(B) She made offerings on a regular basis

(C) Her loyalty to Joseph was exemplary

(D) She was from the right family to fulfill Old Testament prophecy

The Bible or the Bard?

William Shakespeare lived from 1564 until 1616. The King James Bible was published in 1611. So the language is similar. See if you can tell which of the following quotes came from the King James Bible and which were from the pen of the Bard.

---

(1) "The devil can cite Scripture for his purpose."

(2) "Be sober, be vigilant; because your adversary the devil, as a roaring lion, walketh about, seeking whom he may devour."

(3) "This thy stature is like to a palm tree, and thy breasts to clusters of grapes. I said, I will go up to the palm tree, I will take hold of the boughs thereof."

(4) "Who hath woe? Who hath sorrow? Who hath contentions? Who hath babbling? Who hath wounds without cause? Who hath redness of eyes? They that tarry long at the wine; they that go to seek mixed wine. Look not thou upon the wine when it is red, when it giveth its color in the cup, when it moveth itself aright. At the last it biteth like a serpent, and stingeth like an adder. Thine eyes shall behold strange women, and thine heart shall utter perverse things."

(5) "The venom clamors of a jealous woman poison more deadly than a mad dog's tooth."

(6) "God defend the right!"

(7) "His horns are like the horns of unicorns; with them he shall push the people together to the ends of the earth."

(8) "Truth hath a quiet breast."

(9) "Eat no onions nor garlic, for we are to utter sweet breath."

(10) "He hath a heart as sound as a bell, and his tongue is the clapper; for what his heart thinks his tongue speaks."

(11) "Though I look old, yet I am strong and lusty; for in my youth I never did apply hot and rebellious liquors in my blood."

(12) "For scarcely for a righteous man will one die; yet peradventure for a good man some would even dare to die."

(13) "Behold, I have made thy face strong against their faces, and thy forehead strong against their foreheads. Like an adamant harder than flint have I made thy forehead: fear them not, neither be dismayed at their looks, though they be a rebellious house."

(14) "I hate ingratitude more in a man than lying, vainness, babbling drunkenness, or any taint of vice whose strong corruption inhabits our frail blood."

(15) "And whatsoever mine eyes desired I kept not from them. I withheld not my heart from any joy. . . . Then I looked on all the works that my hands had wrought, and on the labour that I had laboured to do: and, behold, all was vanity and vexation of spirit, and there was no profit under the sun."

(16) "Hath my master sent me to thy master, and to thee, to speak these words? Hath he not sent me to the men who sit on the wall, that they may eat their own dung, and drink their own piss with you?"

Answer Key

CHAPTER 1: IDENTIFY THE QUOTE

(1) Bible: Job 19:20 KJV

(2) Shakespeare: *The Merchant of Venice,* act IV, scene i, line 184

(3) Bible: Jeremiah 13:23 KJV

(4) Shakespeare: *A Midsummer-Night's Dream,* act III, scene ii, line115

(5) Bible: Ecclesiastes 3:1 KJV

(6) Benjamin Franklin (Borrowing from Aesop: "The gods help them that help themselves.")

(7) Alexander Pope (Borrowing from Plutarch: "For to err in opinion, though it be not the part of wise men, is at least human.")

(8) Bible: Acts 20:35 KJV (Paul quotes Jesus as saying this, but the quote is not included in any of the Gospels or elsewhere in the Bible.)

(9) Bible: Matthew 7:12 KJV

(10) Alexander Pope

(11) Bible: Proverbs 16:18 KJV

(12) Alexander Pope

(13) Bible: 1 Timothy 6:10 KJV

(14) Bible: Proverbs 22:6 KJV

(15) Samuel Butler (Although give yourself credit if you chose Bible. Butler's quote may be based on Proverbs 13:24: "He who spares the rod hates his son, but he who loves him is careful to discipline him.")

CHAPTER 2: IT'S A MIRACLE!

(1) B [Daniel 2]

(2) J [Exodus 14, 17]

(3) K [Acts 28:1–6]

(4) I [Daniel 3]

(5) C [1 Kings 18:20–40]

(6) M [Judges 15:15–19]

(7) E [Judges 7]

(8) N [1 Samuel 12:16–18]

(9) A [Exodus 7:10, 19–20; 8:5–6, 16–17]

(10) L [Acts 12:1–19]

(11) F [2 Kings 20:1–11]

(12) H [Joshua 10:9–14]

(13) D [2 Kings 4:8–6:7; 13:20–21]

(14) G [Acts 3:1–10]

CHAPTER 3: WHO KNOWS HIS MOSES?

(1) C [Exodus 12:40–41]

(2) D [Exodus 2:3—The word interpreted "basket" is the same in Hebrew as the one used for Noah's "ark."]

(3) D [Exodus 2:11–15]

(4) B [Exodus 2:21–22; 3:1–10; 18:2–4]

(5) C [Exodus 3:10]

(6) A [Exodus 4:1–9]

(7) C [Exodus 5:4–9]

(8) C [Exodus 7:14–11:10—The ten plagues were: water turned to blood, frogs, gnats, flies, disease on livestock, boils, hail, locusts, darkness, and death of the firstborn.]

(9) C [Exodus 12:24–28]

(10) D [Exodus 12:17–20, 33–38; 13:19]

(11) A [Exodus 13:21–22]

(12) B [Exodus 14:25]

(13) D [Exodus 16:15, 31]

(14) D [Exodus 15:22–27; 17:1–7; Numbers 20:1–11]

(15) D [Exodus 32:1]

(16) C [Exodus 32:2–4]

(17) B [Numbers 13:23]

(18) C [Numbers 13–14]

(19) A [Numbers 20:12; Deuteronomy 32:48–52]

(20) C [Numbers 12:3]

CHAPTER 4: NOT A HANDSOME FELLOW

(1) K [Mark 5:4–5]

(2) D [Genesis 49:14]

(3) F [Job 2:7–8]

(4) H [Luke 16:20–21]

(5) L [2 Samuel 21:20]

(6) B [Genesis 25:25]

(7) E [Isaiah 53:2–3]

(8) C [Genesis 16:12]

(9) J [Matthew 23:27]

(10) I [Daniel 4:33]

(11) A [Genesis 4:11–12]

(12) G [John 11:39, 44]

CHAPTER 5: WE THREE KINGS

(1) David (2 Samuel 11)

(2) David [1 Samuel 13:13–14; 16: 7, 13]

(3) Saul [1 Samuel 9:2]

(4) Solomon [1 Kings 6–8]

(5) Saul [1 Samuel 14:24, 43–45]

(6) Solomon [1 Kings 3:4–5]

(7) Solomon [1 Kings 11:1–11]

(8) Saul [1 Samuel 10:9–11; 18:10–11]

(9) Saul [1 Samuel 14:1–14]

(10) David [1 Chronicles 21:16]

(11) Solomon [1 Kings 10:26–27]

(12) David [2 Samuel 6:16–23]

(13) Saul [1 Samuel 10:1–2]

(14) Solomon [1 Kings 3:16–28]

(15) Saul [1 Samuel 28:4–25; 31:1–6]

(16) David [2 Samuel 13:1–22; 15:10–14]

(17) David [1 Kings 1:1–4]

(18) Solomon [1 Kings 4:34]
(19) Saul [David is credited with almost half the Psalms, and Solomon with Psalms 72 and 127.]
(20) Solomon [Matthew 6:28–29]

CHAPTER 6: COMPLETE THE PSALM
(All Bible references are from the book of Psalms)
(1) B [1:1]
(2) C [3:1, 7]
(3) A [6:1, 6]
(4) D [9:19–20]
(5) A [11:5–6]
(6) D [13:1]
(7) D [14:1]
(8) C [18:7]
(9) B [19:14]
(10) A [23:4]
(11) A [24:3–4]
(12) D [38:4–5]
(13) B [46:1]
(14) C [73:1–3]
(15) D [80:4–5]
(16) B [84:10]
(17) D [90:10]
(18) A [127:1]
(19) C [137:1–3]
(20) B [139:23–24]

CHAPTER 7: MAY I HAVE YOUR ATTENTION, PLEASE?
(1) C [Numbers 22:21–35]
(2) N [Exodus 3:1–6]
(3) P [Genesis 11:5–9]
(4) F [Acts 2:1–12]
(5) T [Luke 1:8–22, 57–64]

(6) R [1 Samuel 3:1–10]
(7) G [1 Kings 19:11–13]
(8) L [Numbers 27:18–23] or E [1 Samuel 23:9–12] or A [Exodus 28:29–30]
(9) Q [Jonah 1:7] or F [Acts 1:21–26]
(10) J [Exodus 13:21–22]
(11) D [Daniel 5:1–6, 25–28]
(12) O [Acts 9:1–4]
(13) M [Genesis 19:15–17]
(14) H [Judges 6:36–40]
(15) E [2 Samuel 5:23–25]
(16) K [Genesis 28:10–19]
(17) S [Daniel 3:19–30]
(18) A [Numbers 17]
(19) B [1 Kings 17:1; 18:1]
(20) I [2 Kings 20:1–11]

CHAPTER 8: COMPLETE THE PROVERB
(All Bible references from the book of Proverbs)
(1) B [1:7]
(2) A [3:5–6]
(3) C [6:27–29]
(4) C [10:26]
(5) D [11:22]
(6) B [12:4]
(7) C [12:15]
(8) B [12:24]
(9) C [13:24]
(10) D [14:12]
(11) D [14:30]
(12) A [15:1]
(13) C [16:18]
(14) B [17:12]
(15) D [21:9]
(16) C [22:6]

(17) D [24:26]
(18) D [25:21–22]
(19) A [27:14]
(20) A [27:17]

CHAPTER 9: DREAMS AND VISIONS

(1) O [Matthew 27:19–20]
(2) H [Genesis 37:5–11]
(3) E [Isaiah 6:1–8]
(4) G [Book of Revelation]
(5) F [Genesis 28:10–22]
(6) C [Daniel 7–12]
(7) A [Genesis 15]
(8) K [Acts 16:9–10]
(9) R [Matthew 2:7–12]
(10) N [Genesis 40:16–22]
(11) D [Ezekiel 1]
(12) J [Daniel 2]
(13) Q [1 Kings 3:4–15]
(14) I [Matthew 2:13–18]
(15) M [Genesis 41:1–40]
(16) B [Acts 9:10–19]
(17) P [1 Samuel 3:1–18]
(18) L [Acts 10:9–48]

CHAPTER 10: THE WRITING PROPHETS

(1) M [Zephaniah 1:7–18]
(2) D [Daniel 6–12]
(3) K [Nahum 3:18–19]
(4) J [Micah 5:2; Matthew 2:1–6]
(5) B [Jeremiah 29:10–11; 36–38]
(6) E [Hosea 3]
(7) P [Malachi 3:8; 4:6]
(8) C [Ezekiel 1:15–21; 24:15–27; 37:1–14]
(9) H [Book of Obadiah]
(10) O [Zechariah 5–6; 14:3–4]
(11) F [Joel 2:28–32; Acts 2:17–21]
(12) N [Haggai 1; Ezra 5:1]

(13) G [Amos 7:14]
(14) A [Luke 4:14–21]
(15) L [Book of Habbakuk]
(16) I [Jonah 1; 4:5–11]

CHAPTER 11: SIXTEEN HORRIBLE DEATHS

(1) O [Judges 4:21]
(2) N [Numbers 16:31–33]
(3) P [2 Samuel 6:6–7]
(4) A [2 Kings 2:23–24]
(5) B [Judges 9:52–54]
(6) G [Judges 3:21–22]
(7) L [Matthew 14:3–12]
(8) I [Esther 7:9]
(9) K [2 Kings 9:30–35]
(10) C [2 Samuel 18:14–15]
(11) F [2 Samuel 2:23]
(12) H [1 Samuel 4:18]
(13) J [Acts 12:21–23]
(14) D [1 Kings 22:29–40]
(15) E [Acts 5:1–11]
(16) M [Acts 1:18]

CHAPTER 12: THE ORIGINAL CHRISTMAS STORY

(1) B [Malachi 4:5–6; Luke 1:13–17; Matthew 17:10–13]
(2) C [Micah 5:2]
(3) A [Luke 1:26–27]
(4) C [Luke 1:19–20]
(5) D [Luke 1:7]
(6) C [Luke 1:26–27]
(7) D [Matthew 1:18–19]
(8) A [Luke 1:26, 30–31; 2:21]
(9) B [Luke 2:1–5]
(10) D [Luke 2:7]
(11) A [Luke 2:8–14]
(12) B [Luke 2:12]

(13) C [Luke 2:8–9]

(14) B [Matthew 2:1–11]

(15) D [Matthew 2:11]

(16) D [Matthew 2:11]

(17) D [Matthew 2:16–18]

(18) A [Luke 2:21–38]

(19) B [Matthew 2:13–15]

(20) C [Luke 2:19]

CHAPTER 13: THE LIFE OF JESUS

(1) T [Luke 2:41–52]

(2) F [Luke 3:23]

(3) T [Matthew 3:13–17]

(4) T [Matthew 4:1–2]

(5) T [Matthew 4:4, 7, 10]

(6) F [Matthew 4:18–20]

(7) T [Luke 6:12–16]

(8) F [John 2:13–16]

(9) T Matthew 9:18–19, 23–26; Luke 7:11–17; John 11:1–44]

(10) T [Matthew 8:5–13]

(11) T [Matthew 14:22–33; 8:23–27]

(12) T [Luke 10:1–16]

(13) F [John 3:1–21]

(14) T [John 4:1–26 (especially vv. 17–18)]

(15) F [Luke 4:14–30]

(16) F [Matthew 4:13–16]

(17) T [Matthew 8:14–17]

(18) F [Mark 3:17]

(19) T [Matthew 11:19]

(20) T [Luke 8:1–3]

(21) F [Mark 5:1–20]

(22) T [Luke 8:41–48]

(23) T [Matthew 14:13–21; 15:29–38]

(24) T [Matthew 15:21–28]

(25) T [Matthew 17:1–8; Luke 9:28–36]

(26) T [John 11:53–54; 12:10–11]

(27) F [Luke 17:11–19]

(28) T [Mark 9:33–37; Matthew 20:20–28]

(29) F [Matthew 21:18–22]

(30) F [John 13:1–17]

CHAPTER 14: THE TEACHINGS OF JESUS

(1) T [Matthew 3:1–2; 4:17]

(2) F [Matthew 5:5]

(3) T [Matthew 5:20]

(4) T [Matthew 5:13–16]

(5) F [Matthew 5:17–18]

(6) T [Matthew 5:21–22]

(7) T [Matthew 6:9–13]

(8) T [Matthew 7:12]

(9) F [Mark 4:10–12]

(10) F [Matthew 7:13–14]

(11) T [Luke 16:1–8; 18:2–8]

(12) T [John 6:53–66]

(13) F [Matthew 18:1–5]

(14) T [Luke 10:25–37]

(15) T [Luke 14:25–35]

(16) F [Luke 15:11–32]

(17) T [Luke 16:19–31]

(18) T [Mark 12:28–31]

(19) F [Matthew 24:36–42]

(20) T [John 14:5–14]

CHAPTER 15: JESUS' DEATH AND RESURRECTION

(1) A [Isaiah 53:5,7,9,12]

(2) C [Matthew 26:1–5]

(3) D [Luke 22:7–13]

(4) A [John 13:21–30]

(5) D [Matthew 26:36–46]

(6) C [Matthew 26:49]

(7) A [John 18:4–11]

(8) B [Matthew 26:62–68]

(9) C [Matthew 26:57;
Luke 23:3–12; John 18:12–14]

(10) D [Matthew 21:1–11]

(11) B [John 19:12–16]

(12) A [Matthew 27:19]

(13) C [Matthew 27:38]

(14) A [John 19:19–22]

(15) B [Luke 23:34, 39–43, 46;
John 19:26–27]

(16) A [Matthew 27:46;
Psalm 22:1]

(17) D [Matthew 27:50–53]

(18) D [Matthew 27:57–60;
Mark 15:43]

(19) A [John 19:38–40]

(20) B [John 19:17]

(21) C [Luke 24:1–8]

(22) A [Luke 24:1–12]

(23) C [John 20:10–18]

(24) A [Luke 24:36–43]

(25) D [Acts 1:3]

CHAPTER 16: A BAKER'S DOZEN OF DISCIPLES

(1) M [John 11:16; 20:24–28]

(2) K [Matthew 14:28–31;
26:69–75]

(3) A [John 1:35–42]

(4) B [Mark 3:17; Acts 12:1–2]

(5) D [John 13:22–23]

(6) J [John 12:20–22; 14:8–14]

(7) I [John 1:44–51]

(8) G [Matthew 9:9]

(9) C [Mark 3:16–19]

(10) L [Matthew 10:4]

(11) F [Mark 3:18; Luke 6:12–16]

(12) E [John 12:4–6; 13:29]

(13) H [Acts 1:21–26]

CHAPTER 17: SOUND BYTES

(1) N [Luke 1:34]

(2) I [Job 2:9]

(3) O [Numbers 20:10]

(4) U [Ruth 1:16]

(5) V [Matthew 16:16]

(6) E [Esther 7:3–4]

(7) W [Acts 7:56]

(8) J [John 1:26–27]

(9) Q [Nehemiah 2:17]

(10) X [John 20:25]

(11) H [Job 19:25]

(12) A [Matthew 27:54]

(13) M [Joshua 24:15]

(14) P [2 Samuel 12:7]

(15) F [Ezra 10:10–11]

(16) S [Acts 8:30]

(17) Y [Luke 19:8]

(18) K [Jonah 1:12]

(19) L [Genesis 39:9]

(20) R [John 3:4]

(21) G [Isaiah 6:8]

(22) D [1 Samuel 17:37]

(23) C [Matthew 14:8]

(24) T [John 19:15]

(25) B [Daniel 1:12–13]

CHAPTER 18: THE LIFE OF PAUL

(All Bible references are from the
book of Acts.)

(1) F [The reason for Paul's name
change from Saul is never
explained in the Bible. Many

think he simply adopted a more Greek-sounding name as he took his ministry to the Gentiles.]

(2) T [7:54–8:1]

(3) T [9:11; 21:39]

(4) T [Romans, 1 and 2 Corinthians, Galatians, Ephesians, Philippians, Colossians, 1 and 2 Thessalonians, 1 and 2 Timothy, Titus, and Philemon]

(5) T [22:27–29]

(6) F [22:3]

(7) F [9:1–3]

(8) T [9:8–9]

(9) F [9:10–19]

(10) T [9:23–25]

(11) T [12:25–13:5]

(12) T [15:36–40]

(13) T [14:11–13]

(14) T [14:19–20]

(15) F [15:1–12]

(16) T [16:16–24]

(17) F [16:25–34] (It was Peter who escaped prison with an angel's help—Acts 12)

(18) T [17:22–23]

(19) F [18:11; 19:9–10]

(20) T [19:11–12]

(21) F [19:23–27]

(22) T [20:7–12]

(23) T [21:10–14]

(24) T [21:37–39]

(25) T [23:12–15]

(26) F [24:24–27]

(27) T [25:10–12; 26:32]

(28) T [27:27–44]

(29) T [28:1–6]

(30) F [28:16, 30–31]

CHAPTER 19: THE WRITINGS OF PAUL

(1) T [1 Corinthians 7:10–12, 25]

(2) T [Romans 8:15–17]

(3) F [1 Corinthians 13:8, 13]

(4) T [2 Corinthians 11:23–29]

(5) F [Romans 12:1–2]

(6) T [Ephesians 6:10–18]

(7) T [1 Timothy 1:15]

(8) F [1 Corinthians 5:1–5]

(9) T [1 Thessalonians 5:17]

(10) T [Philippians 4:2–3]

(11) F [1 Corinthians 10:12–13]

(12) F [2 Corinthians 12:2–4]

(13) T [1 Corinthians 14:18]

(14) T [1 Corinthians 15:35–44]

(15) F [2 Corinthians 4:6–7]

(16) F [2 Corinthians 6:14]

(17) T [Romans 9:1–5]

(18) T [2 Corinthians 12:7–10]

(19) T [Galatians 2:20]

(20) T [Galatians 5:22–23]

(21) T [Galatians 6:1–5]

(22) F [Ephesians 1:9–10]

(23) T [Galatians 5:12]

(24) T [Ephesians 2:8–9]

(25) T [Philemon vv. 10–16]

(26) T [Romans 13:1–7]

(27) T [Philippians 1:21–26]

(28) T [1 Corinthians 7:8–9]

(29) T [Philippians 1:13–14]

(30) F [Colossians 3:22–24]

(31) T [1 Corinthians 6:1–8]

(32) F [1 Thessalonians 5:1–11]

(33) T [1 Corinthians 8:9–13]

(34) F [2 Timothy 1:7]

(35) T [Ephesians 4:26–27]

CHAPTER 20: WHERE DO BABIES COME FROM?

(1) B [Genesis 4:25]

(2) C [Genesis 16; 21:8–21]

(3) D [Genesis 25:21–26]

(4) B [Genesis 30:14–16. The shape of mandrakes suggested a human's genital area and so were believed to aid in getting pregnant.]

(5) B [Genesis 19:30–38]

(6) A [1 Samuel 1:12–20]

(7) D [Exodus 2:1–10]

(8) C [Hosea 1:6–9]

(9) C [Genesis 38:8–10]

(10) C [Judges 13:19–21]

(11) A [Luke 1:5–22, 57–66]

(12) A [Luke 1:26–33]

CHAPTER 21: THE BIBLE OR THE BARD?

(1) Shakespeare: *The Merchant of Venice,* act I, scene iii, line 99

(2) Bible: 1 Peter 5:8 KJV

(3) Bible: Song of Songs 7:7–8 KJV

(4) Bible: Proverbs 23:29–33 KJV

(5) Shakespeare: *The Comedy of Errors,* act V, scene I, line 69

(6) Shakespeare: *King Henry the Sixth,* Part II, act II, scene iii, line 55

(7) Bible: Deuteronomy 33:17 KJV

(8) Shakespeare: *King Richard the Second,* act I, scene iii, line 96

(9) Shakespeare: *A Midsummer-Night's Dream,* act IV, scene ii, line 44

(10) Shakespeare: *Much Ado About Nothing,* act III, scene ii, line 12

(11) Shakespeare: *As You Like It,* act II, scene iii, line 47

(12) Bible: Romans 5:7 KJV

(13) Bible: Ezekiel 3:8–9

(14) Shakespeare: *Twelfth-Night,* act III, scene iv, line 390

(15) Bible: Ecclesiastes 2:10–11 KJV

(16) Bible: 2 Kings 18:27 KJV

About the Author

Stan Campbell has more than twenty years of experience in youth ministry, running simultaneously with fifteen years in Christian publishing and eighteen years as a full-time writer. He is the author of more than three dozen Bible-related books for youth and adults. He lives with his wife and son in Hendersonville, Tennessee.